Court Massachusetts. General

Centennial of the Bulfinch State House

Exercises Before the Massachusetts Legislature - January 11, 1898

Court Massachusetts. General

Centennial of the Bulfinch State House
Exercises Before the Massachusetts Legislature - January 11, 1898

ISBN/EAN: 9783744733168

Printed in Europe, USA, Canada, Australia, Japan

Cover: Foto ©ninafisch / pixelio.de

More available books at **www.hansebooks.com**

CENTENNIAL

OF THE

BULFINCH STATE HOUSE.

EXERCISES

BEFORE THE MASSACHUSETTS LEGISLATURE,

JANUARY 11, 1898.

BOSTON:
WRIGHT & POTTER PRINTING CO., STATE PRINTERS,
18 POST OFFICE SQUARE.
1898.

[FROM THE JOURNAL OF THE SENATE.]

JANUARY 6, 1898.

On motion of Mr. CRANE, —

Ordered, That so much of the Governor's Address as relates to the restoration of the Bulfinch State House and the centennial anniversary of its occupancy be referred to a joint special committee, to consist of three members of the Senate and five members of the House; and that said committee be authorized to make such arrangements, and report such recommendations, as may be necessary to provide for the suitable commemoration of these events.

Messrs. Crane, Holden and Moran were appointed the committee on the part of the Senate.

Sent down for concurrence.

Came up, adopted, in concurrence; and Messrs. Lowell of Boston, Harlow of Whitman, Stone of Springfield, Porter of North Attleborough and Cooke of Milford were joined on the part of the House.

JANUARY 10.

A report of the joint special committee who were instructed to make such arrangements and report such recommendations as might be necessary to provide for the suitable commemoration of the centennial anniversary of the occupation of the Bulfinch State House, came up, and was read.

The report stated that the committee had arranged for holding appropriate exercises in commemoration of said event on Tuesday, Jan. 11, 1898, at 11 o'clock A.M., in the present Senate Chamber; that on said occasion His Excellency the Governor would preside and an address would be delivered by the Honorable Alfred S. Roe; and that all members of both branches were respectfully invited to be present at said exercises.

Read and accepted, in concurrence, under a suspension of the rule, moved by Mr. Holden.

The exercises were held as recommended, and were as given in the following pages.

Hon. ELLERY B. CRANE of Worcester, chairman of the special committee having the matter in charge, introduced His Excellency Gov. ROGER WOLCOTT, who presided.

DANIEL W. WALDRON.

PRAYER.

By the REV. DANIEL W. WALDRON,[1] Chaplain of the House.

Our Father in heaven, we come into Thy presence with adoration, praise and prayer. We render homage to Thee as the Supreme Ruler and Lawgiver. We acknowledge that to Thee we are indebted for every good and perfect gift.

Our fathers' God and our God, Thou didst bring to these shores our fathers, who, in prayer and sacrifice, laid the foundations of a great nation, whose rising walls bear witness to the heroic deeds of their sons. We bless Thee for

---

[1] Chaplain Daniel W. Waldron was born in Augusta, Me., Nov. 11, 1840; was graduated from Bowdoin 1862, and from Andover, 1866. Was pastor over Congregational churches in East Weymouth and East Boston. Feb. 1, 1873, became city missionary of Boston, a position still held by him, the twenty-fifth anniversary of which was observed in February last. He preached the last election sermon in 1880, in the Representatives' Hall, the only time an election sermon was ever given there. He was elected chaplain in 1879 and has been re-elected annually since. In 1882 and 1883 Mr. R. M. Bridgman printed a book containing the chaplain's prayers for those sessions, an exceedingly valuable and interesting collection. It contains, also, a list of all preceding House chaplains, with their years of service. Till 1791 the same man acted as chaplain of both branches. Among the seventy-two different men we find that a majority also served as chaplains of the Senate.

the good land we possess; for its civic, educational and religious institutions, from which flow so many blessings to us as individuals, families and a people.

Most gracious God, we are reminded at this hour that our own Commonwealth has always made generous provision for those who have been entrusted with its public affairs and for those who have enacted its laws. A hundred years ago to-day, in solemn procession, bearing valued records and the treasures in the archives of the State, the Legislature came to this building, provided by the generosity of the State and its capital city, and dedicated it to the honor of God and the people's good. We behold on every hand evidence that the men under whose oversight this hall has been prepared for its present use have fulfilled their trust with fidelity, and to like purpose we set it apart this day. Give the wisdom that cometh from above and is profitable to direct to our Senators who are to meet in this chamber, and to our Representatives, as together they endeavor to guard the public interests. Let Thy smile rest upon the homes that nestle among our hills and valleys, send prosperity to our varied industries, and may we become more and more that happy people whose God is the Lord.

Be pleased, heavenly Father, to extend Thy hand in loving benediction upon the Governor of Massachusetts in the discharge of the duties of the position to which he has been called by an appreciative people, to his honorable councillors and to all who hold places of authority and trust.

May Thy favor be continued to the President of the United States, to the national Congress and to all the people of this broad land. Grant that integrity may be the stability of the times in which we live. Help us to put away the sin that is a reproach and to pursue the righteousness that alone exalts. Give protection from every foe. Let justice and brotherly kindness control our relations with other nations.

And now, with holy prayer, the greetings of the chief magistrate of the State and the historic words of the orator, we consecrate this chamber to the promotion of the public welfare. May we also give ourselves to earnest efforts for the good of our fellow men, to willing obedience to the holy and just laws that are a transcript of Thine own mind and heart, and to the endeavor to form such characters as will enable us to leave to posterity the legacy of a good name, when we shall mingle no more in the scenes of earth, and go to pass the final review before Him to whom we shall give account for the deeds done in the body. Prepare us to fight the battles that remain to be fought, to be brave under the trials of life, to recognize the relations that grow out of human brotherhood and that we sustain to our Creator and Redeemer, and at length receive us to honor, glory and immortality in Thy presence.

Hear our prayer, bless us in the services upon which we are entering, guide us in our earthly pilgrimage, and at last may we hear the plaudit, "Well done," dwell in the heavenly mansions, join the "general assembly and church of the first born which are written in heaven;" and to God, the Father, Son and Holy Spirit, shall be eternal homage. AMEN.

ROGER WOLCOTT.

ADDRESS.

BY HIS EXCELLENCY, GOV. ROGER WOLCOTT.

We are met in joint assemblage of the two branches of the General Court, and in the presence of the Governor and Council, to rededicate to the public use of the Commonwealth the stately and beautiful edifice which was, one hundred years ago, in the eloquent words of Governor Sumner, dedicated to the honor, freedom, independence and security of our country. Since then it has been the State House of the Commonwealth of Massachusetts.

Its walls have resounded to the tread and have echoed the words of statesmen, soldiers, jurists and men of affairs, who have had their share in the fame of the Commonwealth. Here have been enacted the laws which have made Massachusetts an example and a leader to the other States of the Union. Whatsoever pride its people may feel in their citizenship, in large measure finds its source within these halls. For a century this building has symbolized the dignity and majesty of the Commonwealth.

Its corner-stone was laid by Samuel Adams, the great popular leader of the Revolutionary period, and by Paul Revere, skilful mechanic and immortal patriot. Its design was the work of Charles Bulfinch, the foremost architect of his time in America, and it stands to-day his most worthy monument.

Either as owner of the site, or as official occupants of the structure, every one of the signers of the Declaration of Independence from the colony of Massachusetts Bay held close relation with this building. Here Presidents of the United States, from James Monroe to Ulysses S. Grant, have been received and entertained with the honor due their exalted office and the character and achievement which they brought to the performance of its arduous duties. Here Webster has spoken, and Everett and Choate and Sumner, and many another with lesser fame who yet has deserved well of the Republic. Here in honored death lay a Vice-President of the United

PAUL REVERE

States, and a Senator of the Commonwealth who had dared and suffered in her cause. Here have acted and labored the long line of my predecessors in office who have made the title of Governor of the Commonwealth of Massachusetts one of the most honored in the nation. Here John A. Andrew gave his heart's blood to the cause of union and nationality. From yonder steps have marched to death or victory the gallant youth of the State, ready to give their lives to a great cause. Here year by year have successive Legislatures patiently wrought to embody in the statutes of the Commonwealth the fundamental principles laid down in the Constitution.

These halls are eloquent with the presence of the great dead. They speak to us with the compelling voice of the past, and bid us be not unworthy of the trust it has imposed. May we meet the problems of the present with the spirit which inspired our fathers, and may we dedicate ourselves anew to the maintenance of a government of the people, by the people and for the people; so may God bless us of this generation as he has hitherto blessed the Commonwealth of Massachusetts.

ADDRESS.

By ALFRED SEELYE ROE.

YOUR EXCELLENCY, MR. PRESIDENT, MR. SPEAKER, AND GENTLEMEN OF THE SENATE AND HOUSE OF REPRESENTATIVES: —

"What is excellent, as God lives is permanent." — EMERSON.

The ink wherewith was written the legislative record of Jan. 11, 1798, as preserved in our archives, shows no trace of fading. There, whoever will may read that on that day, after reciprocal notification by each branch of the Legislature, the various departments of the government of the Commonwealth made a ceremonious march to the new edifice on Beacon Hill. Increase Sumner was then in the first year of his service as Governor, Moses Gill had held the Lieutenant-Governorship nearly eight years, Samuel Phillips was presiding for the tenth year in the Senate,

ALFRED S. ROE.

SAMUEL ADAMS.

and Benjamin Hutchinson Robbins was nearing the end of his fifth term of a like office in the House.

To-day we are realizing somewhat the fruition of the prayers and fervent wishes which from the very beginning marked the progress of this building. With what earnestness had Peter Thacher, of the Brattle Street Church, and an eye-witness of the battle of Bunker Hill, prayed in the Old South Church, where the exercises of the day began, for God's choicest blessings upon this enterprise, July 4, 1795! On that day, when the corner-stone was laid, grand old Sam. Adams, the last of the Puritans, in his executive capacity had expressed the wish that the superstructure might remain permanent as the everlasting mountains. Governor Sumner, a century ago to-day, said: "I am confident that you, gentlemen of both Houses of the Legislature, will cordially join me in the fervent wish that this State House may long remain a monument of the public spirit of the citizens of Massachusetts, as well as a testimony of their respect to our happy political institutions." Six days later, the response to the Governor had these words: "In this splendid specimen of the taste and judgment of the agents who planned and superintended and in the ability of the artificers who completed its structure, we are happy to find the public confidence completely justified. Long may it continue an ornament to the capital, . . . sacred to the purposes to which it has been devoted." As we of this new world reckon time the prayer of Increase Sumner is answered, for the building has long continued. Whether Adams's desire, that this structure shall vie with the everlasting hills in permanency, will be realized, time and subsequent generations must answer. We have done our part.

Since, in 1875, we celebrated, at Concord and Lexington, their respective battles, the people of this Commonwealth have become accustomed to centennials. So prominent have the citizens of Massachusetts ever been in the advancements of the rights of man and in furthering true civilization, that nearly every year brings to the century mark one event or more of almost national importance. Every day is the centennial of something, and from the stand-point of the Infinite, no doubt other selections of objects for distinction than those which claim the attention of our finite minds would often be made. Be this as it may, when a hundred years have passed away since this battle was fought, that man was born, such a ship was launched or this house was built, we like to note the day, and try, therefrom, to gather some impression which may have a profitable bearing on the future.

The intervening century, since the voices of Sumner, Phillips and Robbins were first heard in this hall or chamber, compares favorably in importance with any and all of its predecessors. American affairs were never crystallized. The history of one day is not that of the next. As with a victorious army whose ceaseless cry is "Forward," so in State and nation we have constantly advanced from the camping grounds of yesterday to higher and more commanding positions of to-day. Commerce, mechanics, trade, education, everything that contributes to the good of mankind, have here taken great strides in their advancement, and very few of them have not, in some way, been connected with the edifice whose existence, after the lapse of a hundred years, we celebrate on this occasion. Within these walls must have been discussed, with all possible ardor, the embargo, sailors' rights and the many issues which led up to the war of 1812, our real war of independence. Here Federalist and Democrat fought verbal battles as eloquent as those of their successors in more recent periods. The Missouri compromise and all of the ante-bellum questions had here an airing, and during that memorable period of four years of national struggle, what priceless incidents attached to these corridors and rooms.

In brief, the noteworthy dates in the history of our State House are these: July 4, 1795, when the corner-stone was laid; Jan. 11, 1798, when the formal opening was had; 1853, when the Bryant addition was constructed; 1866, when the Washburn changes were made; 1896, when the late repairs were instituted; and to-day, when we celebrate the centennial. It was fortunate that Charles Bulfinch[1] was the architect. Native genius added to long and devoted study, with foreign travel, had made him the foremost Amer-

---

[1] Charles Bulfinch was born in Boston, Aug. 8, 1763; was graduated at Harvard in 1781; travelled extensively abroad; devoted his life to architecture; died in Boston, April 15, 1844. An excellent life of the distinguished architect, by his grand-daughter, Ellen Susan Bulfinch, was published in 1896 by Houghton, Mifflin & Co., Boston.

CHARLES BULFINCH.

STATE HOUSE FRONT, WITH BRYANT ADDITION.

ican in his profession. The success of this work designated him the designer of the Capitol at Washington, and assured him enduring fame. The building, as he planned it, was symmetrical, elegant and sufficient. Advancing years necessitated changes and modifications. For these he was not responsible, nor were the makers blameworthy. Considering their tasks, Bryant and Washburn did as well as the circumstances would admit. With additions without and alterations within, the edifice gradually grew away from the lines of the original designer, and some, easily discouraged, said, "It is impossible to make the structure take again the form and comeliness of Bulfinch's day." The growth and development of a so-called extension, really an independent building, rendered the preservation of the old edifice extremely difficult. The edict all but went forth that the day of destruction had come, when certain men and women said, "Let us make one more effort to preserve." The result surrounds us. *Esto perpetua.*

"Blessings brighten as they take their flight" is an adage, trite but true. The tablet upon the fence, just below the State House grounds, telling the reader that here once stood the famous John Hancock House,[1] is scant satisfaction, when we reflect how easy it would have been to save the original structure. Its effigy, erected in Chicago at the Columbian Exhibition, was, by common consent, the most interesting and the most visited State building there, rivalling indeed those of the greatest architectural pretensions. Had this edifice been allowed to remain where its builders placed it, who can say what effect it may have had on the present surroundings of this Capitol? Certainly there would have been no necessity of purchasing to the westward for self-protection. Wendell Phillips told us, in his matchless way, that he once escorted a visitor from a southern State beneath this ancient roof-tree; and as the gentleman stepped upon the slab worn by thousands of passing feet, and reflected that through that very doorway had gone so many times the President of the Continental Congress, overcome by his emotions, he said, "You must excuse me, but the presence of so much recalling the venerable past quite unmans

---

[1] This ancient and interesting structure was sold to James M. Beebe and Gardner Brewer, Feb. 18, 1863, for $125,000. It was taken down during that season and the present brown-stone buildings took its place.

me, and I must sit for a moment to recover myself." The same orator, in Chicago, told the people of that boastful city that they did not sufficiently value the first house built within their limits. It was then standing, and could have been retained at very little outlay. "Cover it with glass and gild it with fine gold," said he of the silver tongue, "and it will more than repay the cost." But his hearers heeded him not, and destroyed the most precious object in their midst. When, however, the world was to repair thither to see what Columbia had wrought after four hundred years of striving, Chicago, mindful of her lacking, hurried down to the banks of the James River, carried thence the walls of Libby Prison, brick by brick, and relaid them on the shores of Lake Michigan. She built a *fac-simile* of the home of Robert Burns, and offered fabulous sums to descendants of the poet if they would live therein during the exhibition, just to add interest to the show; but, to the infinite credit of the appreciative Scots, let it be said that they could not be bought nor hired. She even came into our own Bay State, and, in Salem, sought to purchase the birthplace of Hawthorne;

but Salem, a mere mite in the financial world
as compared with Chicago, would not part with
what helps to make her borders so interesting.
The queen city of the west has her glories, but
for history she must await the slow growth of
generations; and when that time comes, will she
have preserved her memorials of Eugene Field
as Massachusetts has hers of Longfellow, Whittier,
Lowell, Emerson, Prescott, Bancroft and
scores of others whom Fame delights to honor?
A resident of this Commonwealth was once returning
from California, *via* the Northern Pacific
Road. As he neared Minneapolis, the party
whose acquaintance he had made during the
long journey insisted on his stopping in the active,
thriving city of the north-west, to see what
great buildings were there. "Do you think,"
said he, "we have no overgrown structures in
the east? If you will promise to show me the
first building erected within the limits of your
proud city I shall be glad to stop." But, no!
False notions of progress had long before wiped
that away, and only towering sky-scrapers remained
to excite the astonishment of observers.
"However," said the traveller, "as you do have

here the Falls of the Minnehaha, immortalized by the pen of Longfellow, I think I will stop off long enough to see them." Unhappily, the falls were having their mid-summer vacation, so Minneapolis presented very little of interest to him.

Scenery alone will not continue to enchant the traveller, else Americans would never go beyond the borders of their own country. Their land offers, in rivers, lakes, plains, mountains, gorges and natural wonders, all that the rest of earth has to present, and more. Not till centuries have intervened, however, can our woods and waters attract as do those of lands where the hand of man has wrought from the dawn of time. The Palisades of the Hudson, the Dalles of the Columbia, the mighty waters of the St. Lawrence, impress and please; but we turn from them to marvel at the history which flows along with the waters of the Rhine. At this point crossed English Edward in the days of the Crusades; here Charlemagne devised his mighty schemes; and there was the bridge which Cæsar built, — till history is lost in legend and myth. Surely Americans do not encounter the perils of ocean travel simply to see what fashion is doing abroad.

Palaces have little part in their expectations, for we have as grand and beautiful at home; rather we go away to see the traces of deeds that have won renown during the ages; and thus, in the wonderful cathedral in Canterbury, we gaze upon the spot where fell à Becket, and look with thrilling interest on the coat worn by the Black Prince at Poitiers. We care little for the size of London, but we are absorbed in the visible evidences of her history, good and bad. Westminster, with its storied memories, St. Clement Danes, with all that it tells of Dr. Samuel Johnson, and every church through whose long-drawn aisle and fretted vault sound the pealing anthem and the note of praise, has some trophy raised by appreciative memory.

More than any other city in America Boston possesses the halo of history. Annually the list of pilgrims to her shrines increases, till books and guides to point out her storied wealth become a necessity. Years since, a Massachusetts teacher, travelling in Canada, made the acquaintance of people residing in New Jersey. The son was a graduate of Princeton, and his law course had been taken in Ann Arbor. They were cultured and discriminating. They purposed returning to their home by way of Boston, and naturally asked for information as to objects of interest. A list of notables was given, and the day of separation came. Later followed a letter from New Jersey, enthusiastic over the beauties and wonders of the New England metropolis. The only trouble with the visitors was the lack of time to do justice to the occasion. A prophet is not without honor save in his own country, and some of those who care least for what our city has to offer are to the manner born. Faneuil Hall, the Old State House, the Old South and King's Chapel claim the attention of multitudes from abroad, while many whose daily walks lead by them see only obstacles in the paths of trade. Happily such are not in the majority, and sentiment has yet some hold upon humanity. Over and over the same arguments have been used for the preservation of the before-named buildings. This room itself has rung with denunciations and with counter-blasts. Not one of them is standing to-day with the cordial assent of everybody. Sometimes woman has had to come to the rescue, and when she has entered the lists man has invariably withdrawn discomfited. What work was done to preserve the Old South, and how could we get along to-day without it, when we wish to illustrate the value of historic study; yet some can recall the long debates in this building as to whether it should be spared, or not. Standing in yonder doorway was a representative,[1] afterward an honored justice of our superior court, when a destructionist was making his familiar remarks on the desirableness of ringing out the old and of ringing in the new; the value of the site of the ancient edifice for business purposes; whereupon the subsequent judge repaired to his own seat, and thence addressing the Chair, in just one sentence, uttered in his characteristically hesitating manner, effectually disposed of all opposition. These were his words: "Mr. Speaker, as near as I can make out, the whole trouble with these folks is they aren't willing that God Almighty should have a corner lot." In spite of opposition, however excited, long and bitter, these buildings, to paraphrase the words of the dying Webster, still exist; and to-day we

---

[1] Charles P. Thompson of Gloucester, member of the House in 1871-72, later a judge of the superior court.

PRESENT SENATE CHAMBER.— Looking North.

PRESENT SENATE CHAMBER.— From Gallery.

add to their number, fresh from the hand of the rehabilitator, old yet new, in all its glory of years and associations, the Bulfinch State House.

"What is there in this building to excite the admiration of mankind?" is a question often heard during the past four years; and, in evidence of lack of appreciation, I think it can be paralleled only by the query of a Representative, sitting in the fifth division in 1894, when it was proposed to do away with the legal features of Fast Day and to substitute therefor the 19th of April. It was then that this citizen, Representative of our Commonwealth, in deep distress over the loss of a day which he had never observed, cried out, "And what ever happened on the 19th of April?" If to those who are familiar with the story of our State House it seems trite and uninteresting, it is not so to many who come to us from abroad. When, in 1895, the Knights Templars of America assembled in Boston, one of the Sir Knights climbed Beacon Hill, filled with a desire to look upon scenes that carry the observer back to the days of the Adamses and Webster. When he found the gates and approaches closed, and "No Admission" greeted his gaze, it was no consolation to him to learn that the extension was open. In forcible if not elegant language he remarked that he wouldn't give a —— to see that or any new building: "I want to see the room in which Andrew worked, the hall where Webster spoke and the chamber where Henry Wilson presided." In 1895, when the fate of the edifice was still in the balance, a resident of far-away Chicago came hither with a friend, who, I am happy to state, has had much to do with the preserving of the structure, and with him went over and through many of the interesting parts of the building. "And do I understand," said he, "that Massachusetts people are going to permit the destruction of this Capitol? If they do, all I have to say is this, just give us folks of Chicago a chance, and we will buy it and remove it, piece by piece, as we did Libby Prison, and we will put it up in our own city as the very choicest relic there." Happily the opportunity did not come to the dwellers by Lake Michigan to taunt us with the possession of what should be and is one of our most cherished heritages. But the battle for its salvation was not an easy one. On the one side were ranged selfish interest, opportunity for still further appropriation of money, a wholly false notion that gaudy colors and glittering tinsel are better than that which has withstood the test of time and which has the impress of genuine genius. The old was derided, the new extolled. Minute imperfections in the ancient were magnified, while defects in the new were ignored. "To be or not to be" seemed the vital question during at least two sessions of the Legislature. The ultimate decision was deferred till the very last moment, during the session of 1896, and was finally made in favor of preservation. "But carry out the plans of the special committee of experts of 1895," said the lamented Greenhalge, "and the Bulfinch front will stand five hundred years." Acting on this suggestion, a bill was framed, giving the direction of repairs into the hands of the Acting Governor, since Governor of the Commonwealth, His Excellency Roger Wolcott; the President of the Senate, the Hon. George P. Lawrence of North Adams; and the Speaker of the House, the Hon. George v. L. Meyer of Boston. The placing of the work in the care of its friends was wholly intentional, and the wisdom of the measure is seen in the results.

After due consideration, the architects employed were Charles A. Cummings, Robert D. Andrews and Arthur G. Everett, of whom the last named has attended personally to the details of the work. The builders have been Messrs. Woodbury & Leighton. Supervisors, architects and builders all vied with each other in carrying out the purposes of the Greenhalge commission. And how have they succeeded? They were told that the sum of money asked for was insufficient, but it has sufficed to restore and furnish, and, what is stranger still, have a surplus to turn back into the treasury. For more than a twelvemonth these halls seemed a veritable land of desolation. The walls were underpinned; mezzanine floors were removed; a steel framework, from the ground up, was made to support the new steel roof; and in the dome iron was made to do the work hitherto performed by wood, till at last "fire-proof" was written over all its surface, within and without. Steadily the work progressed, with no halting whatever, till the building, as designed by Charles Bulfinch, appeared in all its original symmetry and beauty. Never had walls been more severely tested. In the introduction of chimneys and in the making of flues unexpected strains were put upon them. In the effort to detect imperfections these same walls had been almost honeycombed in places, yet the work of the last century gloriously withstood the assaults of both friend and foe, and is good for many a year to come.

It would be an injustice to leave this part of our subject without reference to the aid received from outside sources. Preserved in the archives of the Commonwealth is probably one of the choicest collections of petitions ever presented to the General Court. They came from the State of Maine, signed by the Governor of that daughter of Massachusetts; from Chicago, bearing the names of her most distinguished citizens, many of them natives of the Bay State; from the State Board of Trade; from the architects of America; from labor organizations; from patriotic societies, — till their names became legion. Faneuil Hall and the Old South resounded with the demand for preservation. As one gentleman remarked, there had been nothing like it since the days of the Civil War. The press of the Commonwealth, almost to a paper, supported the proposition. The farmers came in as they did at Lexington, till at last one legislator surrendered, saying, "If the people want it, why let them have it." Poetry was invoked, and a rhymster from the Cape thus remarked: —

> "If the Old State House is out of style,
>   then so is Funuel Hall;
> The Common, too, and Bunker Hill's old
>   monument so tall.
> About their looks, no matter; I know that
>   I'm just queer
> Enough to be right glad and proud to see
>   them once a year."

The New York "Sun" wisely commented, "A single scale of the tutelar codfish is worth a hundred thousand new State Houses."

But the most valuable aid of all was rendered by a committee of ladies, whose chairman was Mrs. Sarah Lowell Blake; the secretary, Lucy Lowell. Right diligently did they labor, and all who applaud the results should unite in praise of these loyal, tireless women. Coming within a year of the return of the Bradford manuscript, now awarded the post of honor in our library, this celebration of ours over an original edifice seems quite in place. Reprints of the manuscript, on the very same lines, are soon to be given away by the State. How should we regard the building itself, not an imitation?

"What is all this worth?" I seem to hear some unconverted iconoclast still inquire. Have you not substituted iron for wood, and have you not changed the material of the columns in Doric Hall? To such queries we must answer, Yes; but no changes have been made not necessitated by the demands of modern building and not necessary to the safety of the structure. No one believes that the famous hall of William Rufus, made familiar to every school boy through the matchless essay of Macaulay on the trial of Warren Hastings, is just as that early British monarch left it. Still, its roof is the finest of its kind in existence, and he would be a bold Briton who, for a moment even, would counsel its demolition, simply because it stands adjacent to the later and more showy Parliament building. Our State House, in its record, connects directly with that of the still older edifice on State Street, so that for quite one hundred and fifty years we can see where the laws of Massachusetts have been made. This Capitol is one of the very few still standing in America that point to the story of a century. Connecticut erected a new and magnificent structure in Hartford, but she did not tear down the old one. That still does duty in the very heart of that beautiful city. Rhode Island is laying out a large sum of money on a building which shall take the place of the two Capitols now standing in Providence and Newport; and in answer to a query as to the probable disposition of the old structure in the former city, a gentleman long the Secretary of State in Rhode Island replied as follows: —

PROVIDENCE, R. I., April 28, 1898.

MY DEAR SENATOR: — Our present State House was erected in 1762 or thereabouts. The new structure is going up in a different locality, and will not probably be completed for some years. Meanwhile, the old edifice is being used. What will be done with it has not been decided. In fact, so far as I know, that matter has not been discussed. There is no doubt, I think, that it will be preserved for some purpose, unless fire disposes of it meanwhile. A special Providence seems to have saved the old building and its precious contents.

Sincerely yours,
J. M. ADDEMAN.

Whoever has seen the stately Capitol of Maryland, in the city of Annapolis, will readily recall its graceful proportions; so, when there appeared a settled purpose to destroy our even grander and more dignified structure, "My Maryland" was addressed, that we might know what was the popular feeling there as to the retention of so aged a State House, built before the Revolution, and the Secretary of State was pleased to answer:—

STATE OF MARYLAND.

OFFICE OF SECRETARY OF STATE,
ANNAPOLIS, April 29, 1896.

Mr. ALFRED S. ROE, *Boston, Mass.*

DEAR SIR:— Replying to your favor of the 27th inst., referring to your efforts for the preservation of the old State House at Boston, I would say that the public feeling in this locality is strongly in favor of the preservation of the old buildings around which so many historical recollections cluster.

The proposition is already being strongly urged for the restoration of the Senate Chamber in our State House to the condition in which it was at the time Washington resigned his commission.

I trust you will be entirely successful in your efforts for the preservation of your State House at Boston.   Very truly yours,

RICHARD BALTAM,
Secretary of State.

The pride of the citizens of the Old Dominion, in whatever pertains to her borders, is well understood, by Americans at least; so, though a serious accident soon after the war had precipitated a crowded room of the Capitol with its occupants into the floor beneath, and though many lives were lost in the calamity, yet to the question of the further maintenance of the building the following answer speedily came: —

THE STATE LIBRARY, RICHMOND, VA.,
April 30, 1896.

DEAR SIR: — Our capitol was planned by Thomas Jefferson, and the model, by Clerissault, sent by Mr. J. from Paris in 1785, is still preserved in this library. The corner-stone was laid Aug. 18, 1785, and it was occupied by the Legislature Oct. 19, 1789, when not quite completed.

There is none who clamor for its demolition, and a riot would likely ensue were such an effort made.

Very truly, W. W. SCOTT,
State Librarian.

A. S. ROE, Esq. *Boston, Mass.*

Here, then, is what those having older Capitols than ours think of their possessions. May we not congratulate ourselves that our edifice, still intact, as it has done for a hundred years, still faces the Common where brave Boston boys, in

General Gage's time, persisted in coasting, and that the dome still greets the rising sun and is yet the cynosure of Massachusetts? These are the very walls that in 1861 and 1865 stood back of John A. Andrew when he reviewed brave sons of the Commonwealth as they passed on to do and dare, and die if need be. Down upon the Common yonder is the towering shaft that Boston has erected to the memory of her soldiers, and thereon we see the front of this very structure, the same one that prompted the hand of the sculptor, not one reared on the delusive scheme of similar lines. Opposite is the finest specimen of memorial art in America.[1] It commemorates a scene in front of this edifice on a beautiful morning in May, 1863. There was not an unoccupied inch of standing room anywhere on Beacon Hill. Was not the Bay State, ever foremost, sending to the front the first regiment of colored soldiers raised in a free State, and why should not humanity stand agog? How proud they seemed, those black men by Harvard College graduate led. Blood then quick and exultant in

---

[1] The memorial to Robert Gould Shaw and the Fifty-fourth Massachusetts Regiment, by St. Gaudens; dedicated May 31, 1897.

a few brief months was to stiffen in a mingled clot of black and white 'neath the guns of grim Fort Wagner; but these walls heard the measured cadence of those feet that marched on to death and immortality, and these same century-old bricks echoed back the drum beats of that glorious host. The nation was just a half century old when, before this Capitol, was formed the procession which, Aug. 2, 1826, marched to Faneuil Hall to hear Daniel Webster descant on the worth of John Adams, who had passed to his reward on the preceding Fourth of July. Said an officer of high rank, in the Rebellion: " I cannot think of the destruction of the Bulfinch State House without feelings of the utmost sadness, for there I and all my associates received our commissions. We went up those very steps, and we don't want a stone or a brick disturbed." In Doric Hall many of the flags of the State and nation were presented by the war Governor, and into the keeping of the State, through that same Executive, they were there returned, or rather what was left of them, after the terrible story of war was told.

Still, " No history " is shouted by an irreconcilable, to whom incidents must have the gloss of at least a century to make them worthy of any consideration, forgetting that a similar spirit would have destroyed the Old South and Faneuil Hall long before their exceeding merit had dawned upon our people, and that the generations of the future are to regard the scenes and deeds of the War of the Rebellion much as we esteem those of the Revolution. This whole building is fragrant with memories of the days when Massachusetts was ready, thanks to the energy and foresight of Nathaniel P. Banks and the equal energy and determination of John A. Andrew. It was no half-hearted support of war measures that the Commonwealth gave. From first to last she was, if anything, a little ahead of Washington in the urging of decisive action. A merchant of Boston is said to have been summoned to the State House in 1862, when Union arms were not winning distinguished victories, and on his arrival he found Governor Andrew in the Council Chamber signing bonds, and his greeting to his visitor was to the effect that he, the merchant, must go to Washington. To his objection that he could not leave his business, the Governor finally said, "I command you to go." "Oh, well, then, if you put it that way I shall have to go." "Do you believe in prayer?" said the Governor. "Certainly," was the answer. "Then let us pray," said John A. Andrew, and kneeling there, in that chamber, he poured out his soul to God. To quote the merchant, "I was never so near the throne of God, except when my mother died, as I was then." His errand was to try to prevail on those in authority in Washington to free the slaves, as a needed war measure. After telling his story to President Lincoln, the latter said, "When we have the Governor of Massachusetts to send us troops in the way he has, and when we have him utter such prayers for us I have no doubt that we shall succeed." The Emancipation Proclamation came in September, and again the merchant was sent for. The scene was changed. It was no longer praying, for prayer had been answered, and they were notes of thanksgiving and praise that ascended from that Council Chamber, — a scene that should hallow it forever. Together Governor and merchant lifted up their voices in "Coronation" and "Praise God, from whom all

GOVERNOR'S ROOM.

blessings flow," and closed with a march around the room to the words of "John Brown's body lies a mouldering in the grave, but his soul is marching on." If many thousands of visitors annually climb the stairs of a hall in Lincoln College, Oxford, to see and stand where met the Holy Club of the Wesleys and Whitfield, may we not expect, in the years to come, that tourists, black and white, shall ask of the keepers here, "Where is the place in which the great war Governor prayed and sang on account of the enslaved African?"

All but three of the governors of the Commonwealth under the Constitution have wrought within yonder chamber. Not including those who served as acting Governors, the number is thirty-two. Hancock, Bowdoin and Adams had passed out of office or life before this day, a century since; but could we recall all that the subsequent Executives have done in their chamber, we should have the story of the political history of Massachusetts well in hand. Sumner, Sullivan and Eustis died in office. Caleb Strong came to his position after his service in the United States Senate. Elbridge Gerry went hence to

GEORGE S. BOUTWELL.

State and nation.[1] We must pass over eighteen years before coming to another surviving Chief Magistrate, William Claflin, one of the few business men thus promoted. In so doing we see John H. Clifford, Emory Washburn, Henry Gardner of Know-nothing fame, N. P. Banks, John A. Andrew and Alexander H. Bullock, one of the most polished gentlemen who ever held the office. Following Governor Claflin came William B. Washburn, who resigned to enter the United States Senate, and Thomas Talbot filled out the unexpired term. Then came a single year of William Gaston, then Alexander H. Rice; and some of us will never forget the affecting words of the aged man as he appeared before a committee with reference to the preservation of this very edifice. "I was but a boy," said he, "when my eyes first rested on the distant dome, and never from that day to this have I failed to admire its proportions and to revere what it and the building beneath stand for. I pray you let no harm come upon it."

---

[1] George S. Boutwell was born Jan. 28, 1818. It is a remarkable fact that six other governors of the Commonwealth were born in the same year. In the order of their executive service their names are: Henry J. Gardner, John A. Andrew, William Claflin, Alexander H. Rice, Thomas Talbot and Benjamin F. Butler. Boutwell and Claflin are the only survivors.

Tears were in his eyes and a tremor in his voice as he spoke these words. Then followed Thomas Talbot and John D. Long. The year of varied action under Gen. Benjamin F. Butler will not soon be forgotten. George D. Robinson succeeded, with Oliver Ames and John Q. A. Brackett in order. Many here can still see the scholarly face of William E. Russell, recall his gentle voice, the characteristic smile; and with sadness we follow him down to the wilds of Quebec, on the Little Pabos River, there, eight hundred miles from his home and kindred, to fall upon the sleep that knows no waking. Then came Frederic T. Greenhalge, and he was the last Governor to occupy the chamber before the renovation. His successor, our own Gov. Roger Wolcott, leads the procession back to the haunts of old.

The Council Chamber, could it reveal its secrets, would furnish material for many a discourse; but its sittings are not for the public eye nor ear. Suffice it to say that the names of many men, tried and true, have been found upon its records, and the Commonwealth is not yet ready to dispense with the Governor's Council.

SENATE RECEPTION ROOM, OLD SENATE CHAMBER.

OLD SENATE CHAMBER.

The Green Room, a creation after Bulfinch's day, is now a memory. Tewksbury investigation, woman suffrage hearings and Meigs elevated railroad schemes are all inextricably blended in its associations. A like fate has befallen the Blue Room, on the east side, over the old Senate Chamber. It, too, was a necessity, worked in to give space for the many committees, but was no part of the plans of the original architect. In the revision, or, better, the return, it has no place. The little better than holes in the wall, into which committees were of necessity crowded, in the revived building are not found; rather there is an effort to replace the partitions and rooms as they were originally.

If noteworthy omissions are found in various parts of the edifice, we may congratulate ourselves that the beautiful Senate Chamber remains intact. Few rooms have ever secured warmer words of commendation than this, in which for ninety-nine years the Senate of the Commonwealth had its sittings. Said a distinguished Frenchman, to whom the architecture of the old world was familiar, "Here is something beautiful," and strangely wanting in appreciation must be that soul which is not elevated at the sight of the simple yet perfect adornments of this chamber. Rufus Choate called it the finest legislative room in the world. In the olden times there were fireplaces on the east side, and upon one mantle-piece might be found a box of snuff for popular use; upon the other, a generous collection of camomile flowers for the comfort of honorable senators.

Barring the few weeks spent by the Senate at the beginning of the session of 1895 in the quarters subsequently occupied by the Governor and Council in the extension, the Massachusetts Senate was found in this room during the sessions of the Legislature till June 10, 1896. There are in this chamber to-day men whose fortune it has been to sit as Representatives here when the room was known as Representatives' Hall. It was theirs to assist in the inauguration of the new hall in the later building. The following year they formed a part of the valedictory session in the old Senate Chamber, whence they went in 1897 to the temporary room, ingeniously fashioned out of what is to be the gallery of the Memorial Hall, a place already

SAMUEL PHILLIPS.

destroyed, so that no man may see just where we met for the sittings of that year, and then they come back to this old hall, hereafter to be known as the Senate Chamber. Truly they have known the State House during its transitional period.

For the nonce, however, let us fancy ourselves in the old chamber, hallowed by its century of associations, and see, if we can, the room as it must have appeared when, headed by Samuel Phillips, the Senators of 1798 filed into their new positions. Powdered hair, cues with eelskin ties, gaudy waistcoats and knee breeches, all terminating in enormous silver shoe buckles, were then quite in vogue. The President[1] was a gentleman of the old school, of the same stock which gave us so many distinguished men, himself the benefactor and organizer of the famous Phillips Academy at Andover. For fifteen years

---

[1] Samuel Phillips, the fifth Samuel in the direct descent from the Rev. George Phillips of Watertown, was born in Andover, Feb. 5, 1752. He died there, Feb. 10, 1802. Graduated from Harvard in 1771, he was early drawn to the patriot cause during the Revolution, and for twenty years was a member of the Senate. He was a judge of the court of common pleas, 1781-89, and was Lieutenant-Governor when he died. He will ever be remembered for his distinguished services to the cause of education, for it was through his prompting that his father, Samuel, and his uncle, John, respectively, gave their fortunes to found the academies in Andover and Exeter, N. H. His wisdom directed what they gave and he was himself a liberal giver to the same cause.

he presided over the Senate, by far the longest term ever accorded to any one man, the nearest approach being the career of his relative, John Phillips,[1] who wielded the gavel ten years, or from 1813 to 1823, inclusive. The latter was the first mayor of Boston. From the list of Senate Presidents it is interesting to note that Harrison Gray Otis, Nathaniel Silsbee and Henry Wilson became United States Senators, the latter Vice-President. The position can hardly be called a stepping stone to the governorship, since only one presiding officer, William Claflin, was thus promoted. We may add the name of Samuel Adams, but he never presided in this building, his term being in the older structure of State Street. From Samuel Phillips to George E. Smith, both inclusive, fifty-two men have presided in this edifice, though the latter not in the old chamber. During these years, under the Constitution, nearly two thousand men have had the right to prefix Honorable to their names through service

---

[1] John Phillips was born in Boston, Nov. 26, 1770, and died there, May 23, 1823. He was graduated from Harvard in 1788, and became a lawyer. He was a member of the Senate nineteen years, dying in office. As the father of Wendell Phillips, he is entitled to enduring fame.

as Senators. In the earlier times it was common for men to be elected to both branches at the same time, and they could then take their choice. In those days mails were slow, and one man, coming down from the western part of the State, presented his certificate of election to the House, was sworn in and assigned a seat. Later came delayed credentials as a Senator-elect, whereupon he presented the same, and claimed the privilege of being sworn in. A debate, lasting two days, followed as to whether he could be sworn in twice in the same session; and the decision was against him, it being ruled that he had already made his selection when he was admitted to the House. To look through the list of Senators during these years would be to read the names of some of the most distinguished men who have claimed Massachusetts as their home. The Adamses, Sam., John Quincy and Charles Francis, were here; Charles Allen, of Free Soil Party fame; "Billy" Gray, the merchant prince of Salem; Samuel Hoar and his two sons, George F. and E. Rockwood; Peter Bryant, the father of the poet; Burlingame, Choate, Butler; the

Lincolns, father and son; and a host of others whose names have been sounded far by the trump of Fame.

The necessity of a Senate as well as a Board of Aldermen in our cities has long been a mooted question. In the early days of our nation the matter was debated before General Washington while he was dining with several men of note, he taking the position that the upper branch was a desirable feature in legislation. "But what good does it do, any way?" queries the doubter as to its utility. Says the First President, "I observe that you pour your tea from the cup into the saucer before drinking. Why do you do that?" "To cool it, of course," was the ready and reasonable reply. "That is just the reason that I advocate a Senate," was the General's statement; "much of our legislation needs a deal of cooling." It is well known that for many years the Senate has been stigmatized by some members of the House, when in a petulant mood, as a "graveyard of House bills." Perhaps no more bills proportionally fail in the Senate than in the House, for so many more are reported in the latter place; but when the smoke of action has cleared away, there are few who do not agree that second consideration in either House is likely to be a cooling one and the public is the better for the process. At the dinner given to Stephen N. Gifford, March 10, 1882, after twenty-five consecutive years of service as clerk of the Senate, Ex-Gov. and Gen. N. P. Banks uttered these words: "I take pleasure in saying that, with regard to the variety of the interests discussed, the novelty of questions, the power brought into the discussion of these questions in the Senate of Massachusetts, where in 1874 I was a member, I would be better pleased to have preserved my record in that session than any other part of my life."

The primordial cell has long been the subject of quest by scientists. Everything has a beginning, but that prime cause is oftentimes more a source of wonder than the result. Massachusetts freemen from the onset either spoke for themselves or through their representatives. Two classes of legislators appear to have had a being, but they voted together and had no negative upon each other till 1643, when a final separation came, as the result of so insignificant an affair as a quarrel over a specimen of the *genus sus*, — in other words, a sow. Winthrop, in his history of New England, says: "At the same general court there fell out a great business upon a very small occasion. Anno, 1636, there was a stray sow in Boston which was brought to Captain Keayne, he had it cried divers times, and divers came to see it, but none made claim to it for near a year. He kept it in his yard with a sow of his own. Afterwards one Sherman's wife, having lost such a sow, laid claim to it, but came not to see it, till Captain Keayne had killed his own sow. The noyse hereof being spread about the town, the matter was brought before the elders of the churches, a case of offence; many witnesses were examined and Captain Keayne was cleared." It appears that, not satisfied with the verdict, Mrs. Sherman, instigated thereto by one George Story, a somewhat irresponsible character, carried the matter before the inferior court then sitting in Boston, where, after a full hearing, the captain was again cleared, and three pounds for costs were awarded by the court. Whereupon the captain brought suit against Mrs. Sherman and Story for twenty pounds damages, on account of the report circulated by them that he had stolen the sow, and recovered. Next the matter gets into the General Court, where for the better part of seven days it occupies the attention of the Solons of that remote period. The issue of this tempest in a teapot was the adoption, March 7, 1643-44, of a resolution empowering the separate sittings of the two branches and their independent voting, along with the necessity of concurrent action to warrant the enactment of a law.

The Constitution under which we still act provided for the election of forty Senators, from stated districts; but at the start there was a queer provision, that from this number there should be chosen, by the Senators and Representatives meeting in the same room, nine Councillors, not more than two of whom should come from the same senatorial district. The districts were re-arranged from time to time by the General Court, the number of Senators depending on the amount of taxable property within the district. This qualification disappeared by amendment in 1840. After the Councillors were elected, there were left only thirty-one Senators, and ere long the gentlemen elected to the Honorable Council were wont to decline the honor, thus necessitating their selection from the outside, and the Senate retained a larger number. With the disappearance of the property qualification came the election of Senators by the system in vogue to-day.

Eighteen different men have been clerks of this body, the longest term of service having been that rendered by Stephen N. Gifford, who died while serving his twenty-eighth term.[1] Henry D. Coolidge has been the efficient officer since 1889.

Many Senators of these later days would think our references incomplete were no mention made of the venerable gentleman who for so many years has opened our sessions with prayer. Formerly a Senator, 1869 and 1870, the Rev. Edmund Dowse became our chaplain in 1880. Born in 1813, it may be doubted

---

[1] Stephen Nye Gifford was born in Pembroke, July 21, 1815. His early advantages were limited, but he secured a fair education at the academies of Hanson and Bridgewater. For several years he was a teacher. In 1850 he represented Duxbury in the General Court. During 1851 he was a Boston custom house inspector. He served as assistant clerk of the Senate in 1851; had a similar place in the House during the following year. During that year he was chosen auditor by the Legislature. Again in 1857 he was assistant clerk of the House. In 1858 he began his long term of service in the Senate, ending only with his death, April 18, 1886.

EDMUND DOWSE.

whether any chaplain in any State can show a better record at the same venerable age.[1]

Of course the thread of legislation has run more or less evenly during these many years. There have been acerbities and amenities, and occasionally the repose of the day has been varied by unexpected episodes. Visitors of note have had their introduction and greetings and

---

[1] Rev. Edmund Dowse was born in Sherborn, Sept. 17, 1813. He was graduated from Amherst College in 1836. He was ordained and installed pastor of Pilgrim Congregational Church in his native town in 1838, and there he is to-day, probably the longest settled pastor in the Commonwealth. During all this time he has had no associate in the pastorate, and, in addition to clerical duties, he has been a member of the school committee as well. In 1886 his alma mater honored him with the title of Doctor of Divinity.

In this connection, it will not be amiss to name those who have preceded Dr. Dowse in his office. Nearly every name is a noted one, and worthy of pages of praise; but the list can include only names and dates: —

1 Samuel Cooper, 1780, 1783; dying in office, he was succeeded, the same year, by Joseph Eckley.
2 John Clark, 1781.
3 Joseph Eckley, 1782-1784.
4 Peter Thacher, 1785-1789, 1792-1802.
5 Samuel Stillman, 1790.
6 Jeremy Belknap, 1791.
7 William Emerson, 1803-1806.
8 Thomas Baldwin, 1807, 1811, 1812.
9 Joseph S. Buckminster, 1808-1810.
10 John Lothrop, 1813-1815.
11 Francis Parkman, 1816, 1817.
12 Henry Ware, Jr., 1818
13 John G. Palfrey, 1819, 1820.
14 John Pierpont, 1821.
15 James Walker, 1822, 1823.
16 Daniel Sharp, 1824.
17 Samuel Barrett, 1825.
18 Francis Wayland, 1826.
19 William Jenks, 1827, 1828.
20 Ralph Waldo Emerson, 1829.
21 Howard Malcolm, 1830.
22 Alonzo Potter, 1831.
23 F. W. P. Greenwood, 1832, 1836.
24 George W. Blagden, 1833.
25 Chandler Robbins, 1834.
26 Hubbard Winslow, 1835.
27 Nehemiah Adams, 1837.
28 Ralph Sanger, 1838.
29 Wm. M. Roberts, 1839.
30 Daniel M. Lord, 1840.
31 Thomas M. Clark, Jr., 1841.
32 Joseph H. Towne, 1842.
33 Wm. M. Rogers, 1843.
34 James F. Clarke, 1844.
35 John T. Burrill, 1845.
36 Amos Smith, 1846.
37 Austin Phelps, 1847.
38 Cyrus A. Bartol, 1848.
39 Isaac P. Langworthy, 1849.
40 Jas. I. T. Coolidge, 1850.
41 Andrew L. Stone, 1851.

have gone hence with recollections of our chamber and occupants. One of these scenes has a particularly vivid place in the memories of some. It was April 27, 1896, the birthday of General Grant. Three men were introduced to us. All were here on account of Grant's natal day. Two are Senators of the United States from the west, the third is General James Longstreet from Georgia, a Confederate leader, second to Robert E. Lee only. He was one of the few soldiers of the lost cause who, when the war was done, not only laid down their arms, but actually ceased fighting. To the observer, seeing only the present, there appeared a tall man with somewhat stooped shoulders, whose blanched locks and face told of nearly four-score years

42 Warren Burton, 1852.
43 J. S. D. Farnsworth, 1853.
44 A. H. Burlingham, 1854.
45 Lyman Whiting, 1855.
46 Daniel C. Eddy, 1856.
47 John P. Cleveland, 1857.
48 Arthur B. Fuller, 1858.
49 Jacob B. Manning, 1859.
50 Joseph Marsh, 1860.
51 Alfred S. Patton, 1861.
52 Edward W. Clark, 1862, 1863.
53 Alonzo A. Miner, 1864.
54 George E. Ellis, 1865.
55 James B. Miles, 1866.
56 Charles E. Reed, 1867.
57 Henry Morgan, 1868.
58 Edward N. Kirk, 1869.
59 John O. Means, 1870.
60 Samuel W. Foljambe, 1871.
61 Edward Abbott, 1872, 1873.
62 Alexis W. Ide, 1874.
63 George F. Warren, 1875.
64 Isaac Dunham, 1876-1879.
65 Edmund Dowse, 1880 to date.

Till railroads rendered locomotion easier, chaplains were sought in Boston. For the first sixty years nearly or quite every one was a local clergyman, and since that date they have come from the near regions.

of living; but among the onlookers were some before whom the years of long ago were passing in rapid succession. They saw the grim, silent soldier sitting his steed on Seminary Ridge, Gettysburg, and it was the nod of that head which sent Pickett and his men over that terrible space towards the high-water mark of the Rebellion,— a failure, but the most glorious charge in history. Again they see him transported to the south-west, commanding the left wing of Bragg's army at Chickamauga, and with the observation born of genius, detecting the weak point in the Union lines, they see him hurling Hood and his followers upon the devoted Thomas with such force and fury that none save that rock could resist. Once more the scene changes. It is at Appomattox. The cause is forever lost. Lee has surrendered, and then it is that our own Ulysses takes one of those arms before us, greets the friend of other days, and says, "Jim, how are the folks at home?" Now the great Confederate utters only these few but happy words: "The time was when it was the height of my ambition to capture Boston. To-day I have found it a very easy task, though on somewhat different lines from those of '61 and '65."

The necessary absence from the old chamber, during the repairs, made it evident that enlarged quarters were necessary, and the old Representatives' Hall was assigned as the future location of this branch, and here we are to-day. Possibly if Senators had been consulted they would have taken with them the helmet, sword and drum recalling Bennington and John Stark, the Lexington musket and the British gun captured at Concord; still, surrounded as they are by the faces of former Governors of the Commonwealth, they are fittingly placed. We miss some objects formerly seen in this place. The floor is changed, the seating altered, but the general effect is much nearer that of a century ago than any one of us ever saw before. We lack the codfish, but we reflect that he is in good and congenial company, among old friends, and we wish all concerned long years of mutual enjoyment. For a century fair faces have looked down into this arena from the east gallery, and from that opposite this platform the families of executives taking the oath of office have regarded the scene. In the west gallery have assembled observers to its full capacity. Again they are all filled with the public and for the public's good. The Legislature of Massachusetts has no secret sessions.

Finally the dream of many a loyal Massachusetts heart is made real on this occasion. Gen. Francis A. Walker deemed the effort to destroy little better than profanation, and were he with us, how would his voice join in acclaim over the restoration! The old State House stands, visible from afar —

> "First glimpse of the sailor who makes the harbor round,
> And last slow-fading vision dear to the outward bound."

From the cupola unnumbered thousands will, in the years to come, enjoy the sights there afforded, and the dome, whether gilded or painted, will continue to greet the gaze of sons and daughters of the Bay State as they near this Massachusetts mecca. Its curved surface must have caught the sound of the guns of the "Chesapeake" when brave Lawrence exclaimed, "Don't give up the ship." Like Olivet over Jerusalem, it watches the tides in the affairs of men. It has noted the changes of a century, and is still the most observed of all that Boston has to present; and on this morning I fancy its spirit may have greeted that of the Old South, saying, "I too am getting along in years, but I begin my second century hail and hearty." And then further off a greeting goes to dear Old Faneuil Hall, with the words, "Your sacred relics are now no more safe than mine." With a hearty "Good morning" goes a ringing salute to the monument, on Bunker Hill, "Like you, firmly rooted and securely builded, I am here to stay. Together let us hold the fort."

May the day be far distant when this edifice shall be any less a source of joy and pride to all beholders. May it be to Boston and to Massachusetts what St. Paul's is to London, the Castle to Edinburgh, — a place "Whither the tribes go up, the tribes of the Lord, unto the testimony of Israel, to give thanks unto the name of the Lord."

APPENDIX.

Executive and Legislative Departments of the Government

of the

Commonwealth of Massachusetts.

1898.

WINTHROP MURRAY CRANE.

Executive Department.

His Excellency
Roger Wolcott of Boston,
Governor.

His Honor
W. Murray Crane of Dalton,
Lieutenant Governor.

COUNCIL

District I.
NATHANIEL F. RYDER . . . of Middleborough.

District II.
BENJAMIN S. LOVELL . . . of Weymouth.

District III.
GEORGE N. SWALLOW . . . of Boston.

District IV.
JOHN R. SULLIVAN . . . of Boston.

District V.
HORACE H. ATHERTON . . . of Saugus.

District VI.
ELISHA H. SHAW . . . of Chelmsford.

District VII.
ALLEN L. JOSLIN . . . of Oxford.

District VIII.
WILLIAM B. PLUNKETT . . . of Adams.

Executive Secretary.
EDWARD F. HAMLIN . . . of Newton.

GEORGE E. SMITH.

SENATE.

PRESIDENT.
HON. GEORGE E. SMITH, . . . Everett.

CLERK.
HENRY D. COOLIDGE, ... Concord.

ASSISTANT CLERK.
WILLIAM H. SANGER, ... Boston.

NAME.	ADDRESS.	DISTRICT.
Bailey, Charles O.,	Newbury,	Third Essex.
Barber, Harding R.,	Athol,	Third Worcester.
Bennett, Josiah C.,	Lynn,	First Essex.
Black, William R.,	Taunton,	First Bristol.
Bouvé, Walter L.,	Hingham,	First Plymouth.
Brigham, William H.,	Hudson,	Sixth Middlesex.
Chamberlain, Loyed E.,	Brockton,	Second Plymouth.
Cook, William H.,	Milford,	Fifth Worcester.
Crane, Ellery B.,	Worcester,	First Worcester.
Dallinger, Frederick W.,	Cambridge,	Second Middlesex.
Davis, William W.,	Boston,	Eighth Suffolk.
Fairbank, Wilson H.,	Warren,	Fourth Worcester.
Farley, Joseph D.,	Erving,	Franklin and Hampshire.
Flint, James H.,	Weymouth,	First Norfolk.
Flynn, Joseph J.,	Lawrence,	Fifth Essex.

SENATE — Concluded.

NAME.	ADDRESS.	DISTRICT.
Folsom, Charles F.,	Boston,	Seventh Suffolk.
Gallivan, James A.,	Boston,	Sixth Suffolk.
Gauss, John D. H.,	Salem,	Second Essex.
George, Samuel W.,	Haverhill,	Fourth Essex.
Harwood, Albert L.,	Newton,	First Middlesex.
Hayes, James E.,[1]	Boston,	Second Suffolk.
Hodgkins, William H.,	Somerville,	Third Middlesex.
Holden, Joshua B.,	Boston,	Ninth Suffolk.
Irwin, Richard W.,	Northampton,	Berkshire and Hampshire.
Leach, William W.,	Palmer,	First Hampden.
Mahoney, William B.,	Westfield,	Second Hampden.
Moran, William,	Fall River,	Second Bristol.
Morse, William A.,	Tisbury,	Cape.
Parsons, Henry,	Marlborough,	Fifth Middlesex.
Putnam, George E.,	Lowell,	Seventh Middlesex.
Quirk, Charles I.,	Boston,	Fourth Suffolk.
Roberts, Ernest W.,	Boston,	First Suffolk.
Roe, Alfred S.,	Worcester,	Second Worcester.
Rourke, Daniel D.,	Boston,	Third Suffolk.
Shaw, David B.,[2]	Boston,	Second Suffolk.
Smith, George E.,	Everett,	Fourth Middlesex.
Soule, Rufus A.,	New Bedford,	Third Bristol.
Towle, William W.,	Boston,	Fifth Suffolk.
Whittlesey, William A.,	Pittsfield,	Berkshire.
Williams, Fred H.,	Brookline,	Second Norfolk.
Woodward, Charles F.,	Wakefield,	Middlesex and Essex.

[1] Died February 5.   [2] Elected to succeed James E. Hayes, deceased.

JOHN L. BATES.

House of Representatives.

SPEAKER.
HON. JOHN L. BATES, . . . Boston.

CLERK.
JAMES W. KIMBALL, ... Lynn.

ASSISTANT CLERK.
FRANK E. BRIDGMAN, . . . Boston.

NAME.	DISTRICT.	ADDRESS.
Adams, Austin F.,	3, Worcester,	Barre Plains.
Allen, Rollin M.,	1, Nantucket,	Nantucket.
Allen, Romeo E.,	9, Worcester,	Shrewsbury.
Allen, S. Augustus,	9, Hampden,	Westfield.
Ames, Butler,	27, Middlesex,	Lowell.
Andrews, Richard F., Jr.,	21, Suffolk,	Boston.
Anthony, Julius C.,	3, Berkshire,	Adams.
Apsey, Albert S.,	5, Middlesex,	Boston.
Attwill, Henry C.,	13, Essex,	Lynn.
Bachelder, Thomas C.,	20, Suffolk,	Dorchester.
Balcom, George,	21, Middlesex,	Marlborough.
Baldwin, John E.,	14, Suffolk,	South Boston.
Barnard, Frank W.,	2, Bristol,	Mansfield.
Bartlett, George H.,	5, Essex,	Haverhill.

HOUSE OF REPRESENTATIVES — CONTINUED.

NAME.	DISTRICT.	ADDRESS.
Bartlett, Jonathan B. L.,	24, Suffolk,	Mattapan.
Bates, John L.,	1, Suffolk,	East Boston.
Battles, David W.,	11, Plymouth,	Brockton.
Beede, Charles O.,	12, Essex,	Lynn.
Belcher, Henry A.,	7, Norfolk,	Randolph.
Bemis, George E.,	1, Franklin,	Charlemont.
Bennett, Frank P.,	11, Essex,	Boston.
Bickford, Scott F.,	28, Suffolk,	Boston.
Bisbee, Horatio,	2, Hampshire,	Chesterfield.
Blaney, Osgood C.,	16, Suffolk,	Dorchester.
Bleiler, John,	22, Suffolk,	Roxbury.
Bosworth, Henry H.,	4, Hampden,	Springfield.
Bottomly, Jerome,	6, Worcester,	Cherry Valley, Leicester.
Boutwell, Harvey L.,	11, Middlesex,	Boston.
Boynton, Warren,	22, Essex,	Ipswich.
Breath, Melvin L.,	26, Suffolk,	Chelsea.
Bresnahan, Hugh W.,	13, Suffolk,	Boston.
Bridgeo, William,	15, Essex,	Marblehead.
Brooks, Oscar T.,	1, Worcester,	Athol.
Brown, Charles E.,	17, Middlesex,	Concord.
Bullock, William J.,	8, Bristol,	New Bedford.
Burgess, Albert H.,	13, Worcester,	Fitchburg.
Callender, Edward B.,	24, Suffolk,	Dorchester.
Campbell, Andrew,	9, Hampden,	Westfield.
Carberry, James F.,	10, Worcester,	Worcester.
Carleton, George H.,	4, Essex,	Haverhill.
Chandler, Leonard B.,	8, Middlesex,	Somerville.

HOUSE OF REPRESENTATIVES — CONTINUED.

NAME.	DISTRICT.	ADDRESS.
Chapple, William D.,	16, Essex,	Salem.
Clancy, James B.,	13, Suffolk,	South Boston.
Clarke, Albert,	9, Norfolk,	Boston.
Clerke, Charles S.,	10, Suffolk,	Boston.
Codman, James M., Jr.,	2, Norfolk,	Boston.
Cole, Samuel,	19, Essex,	Beverly.
Connolly, John W.,	9, Bristol,	Fall River.
Conroy, Thomas A.,	18, Suffolk,	Roxbury.
Cooke, Walter S. V.,	10, Worcester,	Milford.
Coolidge, Daniel S.,	4, Middlesex,	Cambridgeport.
Coombs, George W.,	20, Worcester,	Worcester.
Crawford, Fred E.,	14, Middlesex,	Watertown.
Crocker, Thomas W.,	8, Plymouth,	Bridgewater.
Crosby, Alfred R.,	1, Bristol,	Attleborough.
Crosby, Henry V.,	5, Worcester,	Brookfield.
Crouch, Charles S.,	1, Hampshire,	Northampton.
Cullinane, Richard,	7, Essex,	Lawrence.
Curtis, William,	8, Norfolk,	Stoughton.
Dalton, J. Frank,	17, Essex,	Salem.
Davis, Daniel W.,	1, Essex,	Amesbury.
Davis, William R.,	2, Middlesex,	Cambridgeport.
Dean, Charles A.,	29, Middlesex,	Wakefield.
Dean, Charles L.,	11, Middlesex,	Malden.
Denham, Thomas M.,	7, Bristol,	New Bedford.
Donahue, Thomas,	10, Bristol,	Fall River.
Donovan, Eugene E.,	3, Bristol,	Taunton.
Dooling, Thomas J.,	7, Hampden,	Holyoke.

HOUSE OF REPRESENTATIVES — Continued.

NAME.	DISTRICT.	ADDRESS.
Drake, Frederic P.,	4, Norfolk,	Canton.
Draper, Henry J.,	26, Middlesex,	Lowell.
Driscoll, Daniel J.,	6, Hampden,	Chicopee.
Dubuque, Hugo A.,	11, Bristol,	Fall River.
Dumond, John B.,	12, Suffolk,	Boston.
England, Daniel,	1, Berkshire,	Pittsfield.
Estes, Eugene B.,	9, Plymouth,	Brockton.
Estey, Francis W.,	23, Suffolk,	Roslindale.
Farmer, Frank H.,	27, Middlesex,	Tewksbury.
Fartur, Francis F.,	13, Worcester,	Fitchburg.
Favor, John,	20, Essex,	Gloucester.
Fay, Asa B.,	11, Worcester,	Northborough.
Feneno, John J.,	19, Suffolk,	Roxbury.
Fitzgerald, William T. A.,	7, Suffolk,	Boston.
Folsom, Albert T.,	1, Hampden,	Springfield.
Foster, Harry C.,	19, Essex,	Boston.
Francis, Frank W.,	8, Bristol,	New Bedford.
Frederick, George G.,	6, Essex,	Methuen.
Fuller, George F.,	3, Hampden,	Springfield.
Gaddis, Michael E.,	18, Suffolk,	Boston.
Garrity, Richard W.,	17, Suffolk,	Roxbury.
Gartland, John J., Jr.,	9, Suffolk,	Boston.
Gaylord, Henry E.,	3, Hampshire,	So. Hadley Falls.
Gilman, Moses D.,	16, Worcester,	Worcester.
Gleason, David J.,	11, Suffolk,	South Boston.
Gore, Otis M.,	15, Middlesex,	Waltham.
Grant, Oliver S.,	19, Suffolk,	Boston.

HOUSE OF REPRESENTATIVES – Continued.

NAME.	DISTRICT.	ADDRESS.
Grimes, James W.,	28, Middlesex,	Boston.
Hall, Almon E.,	2, Berkshire,	Williamstown.
Hall, Amos E.,	10, Middlesex,	Everett.
Hall, Luther,	2, Barnstable,	Dennis.
Hammond, Frederick,	25, Suffolk,	Allston.
Harlow, Franklin P.,	5, Plymouth,	Whitman.
Harwood, George F.,	14, Essex,	Lynn.
Haskins, Leander M.,	21, Essex,	Boston.
Hawes, Martin E.,	6, Norfolk,	East Weymouth.
Hayes, Alfred S.,	12, Suffolk,	Boston.
Hayes, William H. I.,	26, Middlesex,	Lowell.
Hayward, Albert F.,	16, Middlesex,	Newton Highlands.
Hemphill, Ashton E.,	8, Hampden,	Holyoke.
Hill, John W.,	1, Hampshire,	Williamsburg.
Hiscox, Albert F.,	7, Worcester,	Webster.
Hoag, Charles E.,	5, Hampden,	Springfield.
Holton, Seba A.,	1, Barnstable,	Falmouth.
Horgan, Francis J.,	8, Suffolk,	Boston.
How, Carleton F.,	3, Essex,	Haverhill.
Howard, Walter F.,	11, Worcester,	Clinton.
Howe, Rufus,	22, Middlesex,	Hudson.
Hoyt, Edward H.,	9, Essex,	Haverhill.
Huntress, Franklin E.,	7, Middlesex,	Boston.
Innes, Charles H.,	10, Suffolk,	Boston.
Johnson, Charles R.,	21, Worcester,	Worcester.
Jones, George R.,	31, Middlesex,	Boston.
Jones, Melville D.,	7, Middlesex,	Somerville.

HOUSE OF REPRESENTATIVES — Continued.

NAME.	DISTRICT.	ADDRESS.
Jones, Michael B.,	10, Bristol,	Fall River.
Josselyn, William A.,	2, Plymouth,	North Pembroke.
Joubert, Joseph H.,	7, Essex,	Lawrence.
Kane, Daniel J.,	6, Suffolk,	Boston.
Keith, Charles P.,	1, Middlesex,	Cambridgeport.
Kells, William, Jr.,	15, Suffolk,	South Boston.
Kelly, John L.,	2, Suffolk,	East Boston.
Kenefick, Thomas W.,	1, Hampden,	Palmer.
Kiley, Daniel J.,	8, Suffolk,	Boston.
King, Arthur D.,	2, Hampden,	North Wilbraham.
King, Randolph V.,	22, Suffolk,	Jamaica Plain.
Kyle, William S.,	1, Plymouth,	Plymouth.
Lang, William A.,	25, Middlesex,	Lowell.
Learoyd, Addison P.,	10, Essex,	Danvers.
Leland, Francis,	2, Worcester,	Otter River.
Lewis, Charles D.,	20, Middlesex,	So. Framingham.
Libby, John F.,	12, Middlesex,	Boston.
Lockhart, Alexander,	11, Bristol,	Fall River.
Lyon, Albert W.,	16, Suffolk,	Dorchester.
Macken, Luke J.,	5, Berkshire,	Hinsdale.
Mackey, Thomas,	7, Suffolk,	Boston.
Magenis, John E.,	1, Berkshire,	North Adams.
Mahoney, David A.,	9, Suffolk,	Boston.
Mahoney, William E.,	4, Suffolk,	Boston.
Marden, William H.,	30, Middlesex,	Stoneham.
Mayo, Benjamin W.,	3, Franklin,	Turner's Falls.
McCarthy, Jeremiah J.,	4, Suffolk,	Charlestown.

House of Representatives—Continued.

NAME.	DISTRICT.	ADDRESS.
McKnight, Levi G.,	2, Worcester,	West Gardner.
McLoughlin, William L.,	17, Worcester,	Worcester.
McManus, John A.,	15, Suffolk,	South Boston.
Mead, George F.,	13, Middlesex,	Lexington.
Meek, Thomas H.,	8, Worcester,	East Douglas.
Mellen, George W.,	7, Berkshire,	Great Barrington.
Miller, William J.,	5, Suffolk,	Charlestown.
Mills, Charles P.,	22, Essex,	Newburyport.
Montgomery, James A.,	2, Middlesex,	Cambridge.
Morrison, Andrew H.,	11, Bristol,	Fall River.
Morse, William L.,	21, Middlesex,	Marlborough.
Myers, James J.,	1, Middlesex,	Boston.
Nettleton, William A.,	6, Berkshire,	Stockbridge.
Nevin, Edward B.,	6, Norfolk,	Boston.
Newcomb, Thaddeus H.,	5, Norfolk,	Quincy.
Newcomb, William N.,	4, Hampshire,	Ware.
Newton, H. Huestis,	10, Middlesex,	Everett.
Noonan, T. Frank,	3, Suffolk,	Charlestown.
Norton, George H.,	17, Suffolk,	Boston.
O'Connor, James,	2, Suffolk,	East Boston.
Parker, Charles E.,	4, Worcester,	Holden.
Parker, Harold,	12, Worcester,	South Lancaster.
Parsons, Herbert C.,	2, Franklin,	Greenfield.
Paton, Alexander S.,	14, Worcester,	Leominster.
Pattee, Joseph E.,	26, Middlesex,	Lowell.
Perry, Francis C.,	18, Middlesex,	Natick.
Peters, Lemuel W.,	23, Suffolk,	Boston.

HOUSE OF REPRESENTATIVES — CONTINUED.

NAME.	DISTRICT	ADDRESS.
Philbrick, Joseph M.,	5, Bristol,	Taunton.
Phillips, Franklin F.,	7, Middlesex,	Somerville.
Pickard, Edward L.,	16, Middlesex,	Auburndale.
Ponce, John H.,	3, Middlesex,	East Cambridge.
Poor, Albert,	8, Essex,	Andover.
Porter, Burrill, Jr.,	1, Bristol,	N. Attleborough.
Powers, John A.,	11, Middlesex,	Malden.
Pratt, David G.,	7, Plymouth,	N. Middleborough.
Ramsay, James P.,	25, Middlesex,	Lowell.
Ramsdell, Charles H.,	13, Essex,	Lynn.
Reed, Silas D.,	4, Bristol,	Taunton.
Rice, George M.,	15, Worcester,	Worcester.
Richardson, Frank S.,	1, Berkshire,	North Adams.
Ross, Leonard W.,	25, Suffolk,	Boston.
Ross, Samuel,	7, Bristol,	New Bedford.
Rowan, John A.,	6, Suffolk,	Boston.
Rowell, Edward T.,	26, Middlesex,	Lowell.
Russell, Michael L.,	18, Worcester,	Worcester.
Saunders, Charles R.,	11, Suffolk,	Boston.
Sears, Thomas D.,	3, Barnstable,	North Brewster.
Seavey, James F.,	11, Essex,	Lynn.
Selfridge, George S.,[1]	11, Suffolk,	Boston.
Severance, William H.,	12, Essex,	Lynn.
Sheehan, John F.,	7, Hampden,	Holyoke.
Sisson, Robert S.,	11, Essex,	Lynn.
Skillings, William E.,	21, Suffolk,	Roxbury.
Slocum, John O.,	6, Bristol,	Dartmouth.

[1] Elected to succeed Francis C. Lowell, resigned.

APPENDIX. 73

HOUSE OF REPRESENTATIVES — CONTINUED.

NAME.	DISTRICT.	ADDRESS.
Smart, George B.,	6, Essex,	Lawrence.
Smith, Harvey C.,	20, Essex,	Gloucester.
Snow, Andrew R.,	7, Worcester,	Webster.
Stalker, Hugh L.,	1, Suffolk,	East Boston.
Stanley, Benjamin F.,	2, Essex,	Newburyport.
Staples, Nathaniel G.,	6, Plymouth,	Lakeville.
Stebbins, Marcus M.,	4, Franklin,	Erving.
Stevenson, John M.,	4, Berkshire,	Pittsfield.
Stewart, Joseph I.,	20, Suffolk,	Dorchester.
Stone, Willmore B.,	3, Hampden,	Springfield.
Sullivan, Cornelius F.,	7, Essex,	Lawrence.
Swift, William S.,	1, Dukes,	Vineyard Haven.
Taft, Arthur R.,	9, Worcester,	Uxbridge.
Tague, Peter F.,	3, Suffolk,	Charlestown.
Talbot, Zephaniah,	19, Middlesex,	Holliston.
Thompson, James,	5, Norfolk,	Quincy.
Tilton, Charles W.,	10, Plymouth,	Brockton.
Trow, Charles E.,	18, Essex,	Salem.
Tuttle, Samuel A.,	3, Norfolk,	Hyde Park.
Twomey, Edmund J.,	5, Suffolk,	Charlestown.
Waite, J. Gilman,	9, Middlesex,	Medford.
Washburn, Charles G.,	22, Worcester,	Worcester.
Waterman, Eben C.,	4, Plymouth,	Hanover.
Wells, Abelard E.,	10, Essex,	Peabody.
Wentworth, Edward E.,	3, Plymouth,	Cohasset.
Whidden, George W.,	15, Middlesex,	Waltham.
Whipple, John J.,	10, Plymouth,	Boston.

House of Representatives – Concluded.

NAME.	DISTRICT.	ADDRESS.
Whitaker, Elbridge J.,	10, Norfolk,	Wrentham.
Whitcomb, Frank H.,	23, Middlesex,	West Acton.
Whitcomb, George L.,	24, Middlesex,	Townsend.
White, Horace C.,	6, Middlesex,	Somerville.
Whitehead, James,	9, Bristol,	Fall River.
Willard, Edward E.,	27, Suffolk,	Chelsea.
Williams, Appleton P.,	10, Worcester,	West Upton.
Williams, George Fenelon,	10, Norfolk,	Foxborough.
Winslow, Francis O.,	1, Norfolk,	Norwood.
Wood, Alva S.,	28, Middlesex,	Woburn.

www.ingramcontent.com/pod-product-compliance
Lightning Source LLC
Chambersburg PA
CBHW020124170426
43199CB00009B/623